New Jersey Wildlife

Animals & Mammals

Billy Grinslott – Kinsey Marie Books

ISBN - 9781968228651

Chipmunks are found in many areas. Chipmunks are small members of the squirrel family. They like to eat nuts and seeds. Chipmunks are most active during the day, especially at dawn and dusk. They have pouches inside of their cheeks so they can carry food. They are very friendly and will take food from your hand. Chipmunks need about 15 hours of sleep per day. The smallest chipmunk species is Tamias minimus, which is found throughout North America.

There are many squirrels in the wild. You may see a red or gray squirrel. The most popular is the gray squirrel. Squirrels are very acrobatic and can climb trees. Their favorite food is acorns. Squirrels hide their food in many small stashes and can find more than 90% of them later. Squirrels are fast and can run up a tree at 12 miles per hour. Newborn squirrels are blind, deaf, and hairless, and rely on their mother until they mature.

Flying Squirrels don't fly like birds. They don't have wings. They have skin that is attached to their legs. When they jump from a tree, they spread their legs out and glide through the air. Most glides are 30 feet from tree to tree. But they can glide up to 150 feet. They are primarily active at night and are social animals, often living in groups and sharing nests. They have large eyes for night vision, long whiskers for navigating in the dark, and a long, flattened tail for steering during glides.

Many Lemmings fur can change color with the seasons. Their front paws have broad, flattened claws for digging. Lemmings live in holes and tunnels that they dig in the ground. In winter they tunnel under the snow. Lemmings eat mosses, roots, and grasses. Lemmings are very small animals, usually, just three to six inches long. Their bodies are covered in thick fur, and they don't hibernate during winter months, they are active year-round.

There are many types of rabbits in the wild. The most common is the cottontail. Rabbits are cute, friendly, and fun to watch. Many people have rabbits for pets. They have soft fluffy fur. They are called cottontails because they have a white fluffy tail that looks like a cotton ball. Rabbits thrive in brushy areas, fields, and wooded habitats.

The hare is bigger than a cottontail rabbit with longer ears and legs. Their longs legs help them to run fast. They are agile and faster than most rabbits. Hares have excellent hearing and vision. They have large ears and eyes that are positioned on the sides of their head, giving them a wide field of vision. Hares can change color. They can change color depending on the season and their surroundings.

The black-tailed jackrabbit is a large, long-eared North American hare, not a true rabbit. They are known to run at speeds of 40 miles per hour, they can leap 20 feet in a single bound, and they have distinct, black-tipped ears and tails. Their long 5-to-7-inch ears act as vents and release heat, to keep them from overheating on hot days. Another interesting fact is, they thump their hind legs to signal danger.

Pee-ewe what is that stinky critter with the big bushy tail. It smells bad. Skunks are normally curious and friendly unless you scare them. If you scare them, they will flip their bushy tale at you and spray you with a smelly potion and it stinks. Skunks spray a smelly, sulfur-based liquid from their anal glands as a defense mechanism. The spray can cause eye irritation and temporary blindness. Skunks are highly adaptable and can thrive in many different environments. Skunks have strong forefeet and long claws for digging. Skunks live in dens underground.

Opossums or possums have strong tails and can hang from trees. One trick that a possum has, is when it feels danger is it will play dead. It will lay there and not move. Possums have white to gray face hair. Possums like to eat wood ticks. They are also immune to snakebites. Opossums are susceptible to frostbite because their hands and tails are not protected by fur. Opossums are marsupials, which means they have pouches for their young, like kangaroos and koalas.

Raccoons like to come out at night. Their eyes are made so they can see in the dark. Raccoons are highly intelligent and can solve problems. They can learn to open doors, trash cans, and other containers. They are called masked bandits because they like to raid and eat out of trash cans at night. Raccoons can survive in many environments.

Mallard ducks are by far the most recognizable and popular ducks in the world. They live in just about every area of North America. Their estimated population is around 19 million birds. The male is easily recognizable from its white neck ring and green neck and head. The female Mallard has between five to 14 light green eggs. Most ducks don't have green eggs, so this makes them unique. The male Mallard is called a drake and the female a hen. Female Mallards quack. Males don't quack, instead they produce deeper, raspier one- and two-note calls. They can also make rattling sounds by rubbing their bills against their flight feathers.

Canada Geese are the most sought after and abundant goose in North America. They live in many places. Canada geese can travel 1,500 miles in a day if the weather permits. Canada geese migrate every year. They fly in a V-formation, which allows them to travel long distances without stopping, as they can switch positions and conserve energy. Canada geese are known for their distinctive honk and are sometimes called Canadian honkers.

Grouse, particularly ruffed grouse, are interesting birds known for their unique drumming displays. They flap or rotate their wings, and it sounds like drums beating. During winter, ruffed grouse often burrow into snow. They have comb-like fringes on their toes that act like snowshoes, allowing them to walk easily on snow.

The bobwhite quail has the largest range of any game bird in America. Bobwhite quail are the most common species of quail. The bobwhite is often referred to as the number one game bird of the eastern and southern United States. Bobwhite quail are known for their explosive flight, and social behavior in groups called coveys.

Mourning Doves are unable to sweat. To stay cool during hot weather, they pant just like dog do. Mourning doves eat and collect seeds in their crop, which is an enlarged part of their esophagus. Then they digest them later. It's estimated that there are more than 100 million mourning doves in the US. With the southern states having the biggest population.

Ringed Neck Pheasants are one of the most sought-after birds in North America. They are found throughout most of Northern America and Canada. Ring-necked pheasants are not native to the US. Instead, they were brought here from Asia in the 1880's. While not as widespread as quail, they are present in some areas of New Jersey.

Wood ducks are by far one of the coolest looking birds. Males have vibrant colors and long feathers on the back of their head. Wood Ducks are unique among most waterfowl. They need bodies of water that are near trees. They use lakes, ponds, and streams that are adjacent to wooded areas so they can nest in tree cavities.

The Wild Turkey is a large, bird that is native to North America. It is the heaviest bird in the United States and can weigh up to 24 pounds. Only male turkey's gobble. Wild turkeys can fly. Wild turkeys sleep in trees. Their heads can change colors. You can tell a turkey's emotions by the color of their heads. Colors can change from red to blue to white, depending on how excited or calm they are. You can find wild turkeys in just about every state in America.

Beavers use their teeth to cut and knock down trees. They build dams with them to block water, so they have a place to live and swim. They also eat wood. Beavers can stay underwater for about 8 minutes. Beavers slap their tails on the water to indicate danger. Beavers are the largest rodents in North America.

Otters have the thickest fur of any animal. The otter is one of the few mammals that use tools, like rocks to break thing open. A group of otters resting together is called a raft.

Otters primarily rely on their sense of touch, whiskers, and forepaws, in murky waters to locate food. Otters have built in pouches of loose skin under their forearms to stash extra food when diving.

Nutria are large, semi-aquatic rodents known for their orange teeth and webbed hind feet. They are invasive in many areas, where they can cause significant damage. Their burrowing can destroy riverbanks and levees, and their diet of eating vegetation can decimate marshlands. Nutrias are larger than muskrats but smaller than beavers. Their large yellow-orange incisor teeth are used for gnawing and eating plants. Their partially webbed hind feet make them excellent swimmers. Nutrias have relatively poor eyesight and rely more on their hearing to detect danger. Unlike beavers and muskrats, they have a long, round, and mostly hairless tail.

Muskrats are found in marshes, ponds, and streams with abundant aquatic vegetation. Muskrats have a scaly tail that acts as a rudder for swimming and helps them stay afloat. They primarily eat aquatic plants like cattails, sedges, and grasses, but also consume small animals like mussels, crayfish, and fish. They have a second set of lips that close behind their front incisors, enabling them to dive underwater, chew, and eat without swallowing water. They build lodges made of mud and vegetation and also live in burrows along the banks of water sources.

Groundhogs or woodchucks are the largest member of the squirrel family. Groundhogs get their name because of their big bodies, and they live underground. Groundhogs are skilled climbers and swimmers. Groundhogs are true hibernators, sleeping for up to six months. Groundhog Day is where Punxsutawney Phil predicts how long winter will last.

The American Mink lives across most of North America and is a cat sized. Mink are very skilled climbers and swimmers. They prefer to keep to themselves. They communicate using odors, visual signals, and other sounds. They purr when they're happy, like cats. Mink are agile swimmers, and they often dive to find food.

Weasels are the smallest members of the meat-eating animals. Although small, they do not hibernate and are active all winter. Weasels in northern ranges turn white in the winter to camouflage in the snow. Weasels have long whiskers like cats, to help them feel things. They even have long whiskers on their elbows. When a weasel gets annoyed, it stomps its feet, just like humans do. Weasels are quick, agile, and alert animals. They are excellent climbers and swimmers.

The Stoat or ermine is part of the weasel family. Stoats can thrive in many climates and environments. They can live in most habitats if there's food and shelter. Stoats are opportunistic predators that hunt day and night. They have a strong sense of smell and can travel up to 1.5 miles in a few hours. Stoats are good at climbing trees. They can swim and dive underwater. Stoats can reach speeds of up to 20 miles an hour. In colder climates, stoats turn almost completely white, with just a black tip on their tail.

Fishers live in the forests of Canada and the northern United States. They hiss and growl when upset. They are closely related to badgers, mink, and otters. Fisher young are known as kits. Fishers are one of the few animals that eat porcupines. Fishers are also called pekan, pequam, wejack, and woolang.

Porcupines have sharp quills to help protect them. A porcupine can have up to 30 thousand quills. They are sharp and will stick you if you touch them. Porcupines are excellent climbers with long claws. Porcupines are shy, nocturnal, and solitary animals that spend much of their time in trees. To communicate they make grunts and high-pitched noises. A group of porcupines is called a family.

Gray fox prefers to live in rocky canyons and ridges but can also be found in wooded areas and open fields. They have strong, hooked claws that enable them to climb trees. Which is abnormal for a dog species. Gray foxes are not observed as frequently as red foxes due to their reclusive nature and more nocturnal habits. Gray foxes are small, only weighing 7 to 10 pounds.

Red foxes have excellent hearing, allowing them to hear rodents digging underground from far distances. When afraid, red foxes grin or look like they are smiling. Red fox's front paws have five toes, while their hind feet only have four. Foxes dig underground dens where they raise their kits and hide from predators. A group of foxes is called a skulk or a leash. Babys are called kits and females are called vixens.

The coyote is bigger than a fox weighing between 20 and 45 pounds. Eastern coyotes are part wolf. Coyotes are great for pest control. They like to eat mice and rats. They can adapt and live almost anywhere, even in the city. Coyotes are very smart and have been observed learning and following traffic signals in some cities. They have a yip type of call when they communicate with each other. Coyotes are found in all the United States, except Hawaii.

The Coywolf got its name because it is a cross between the coyote, wolf and dogs. While coyotes are common, they are smaller than wolves. Coyotes typically weigh around 30-40 pounds, while coywolf hybrids can weigh significantly more, with some reports suggesting specimens of over 60 pounds. They can be significantly larger than a typical coyote.

Yes, wild or feral hogs exist in New Jersey, primarily appearing as isolated populations in Burlington County and other areas, where they can damage landscapes and property. Feral hogs are also known as wild boars or wild pigs. Feral hogs are known for their high reproductive rates and their tendency to root up the ground, which can lead to habitat destruction. They are highly intelligent, social animals with a keen sense of smell and a surprisingly good memory. Wild pigs can be found in various habitats, including forests, grasslands, and agricultural areas.

Bobcats are named for their short, bobbed tails with white tips. They have similar markings to lynxes but are much smaller. Bobcats live in a variety of habitats. Bobcats are skilled at leaping and can run up to 30 miles per hour.

Black bears are the smallest members of the bear family in North America. Black Bears love to eat sweet things like berries, fruits, and vegetables. They are good climbers and fast runners. They are excellent swimmers and can paddle at least a mile and a half in freshwater. They usually sleep for long periods of time and hibernate during the winter. They typically try to stay away from people unless they find food in the area.

The whitetail deer is the most popular deer in North America. Whitetail deer have good eyesight and hearing. They can detect small sounds from a quarter of a mile away. Only male deer grow antlers, which are shed each year. Whitetail deer are good swimmers and will use large streams and lakes to escape predators. A young deer is called a fawn, a male is a buck, and a female is called a doe. They are the most common deer species and live everywhere in North America.

Yes, there are American bison in New Jersey, primarily located on private, specialized farms. The most well-known location is the Readington River Buffalo Farm in Hunterdon County, which raises a herd of nearly 100 bison. Bison are the largest mammal in North America and weigh up to 2,000 pounds. Bison can run up to 35 miles per hour. They can jump 6 feet vertically and more than 7 feet horizontally. Bison calves are nicknamed red dogs, because of their orange-red color at birth.

Fun Facts about New Jersey Animals

1 – The official state animal of New Jersey is the horse. It was selected to represent the state's agricultural history, industry, and strength.

2 - Black Bears are the largest land mammal in the state, with populations established in all 21 counties, particularly in the north.

3 - The Opossum is North America's only marsupial. They are the only animals that carry their young in a pouch, like a Kangaroo.

4 - The largest wild cat in New Jersey is the Bobcat. They typically weigh up to 35 pounds and measure 25 to 30 inches in length.

5 - Coyotes are the most abundant large predator, and they usually prey on small mammals, rats and mice. They can adapt to live anywhere.

6 - Extirpated Species: Wolves, and cougars once roamed New Jersey but are no longer present.

7 - The gray fox is the smallest wild canine, member of the dog family.

8 – New Jersey has over 400 species of land-dwelling vertebrates, 336 marine fish species, and 134 freshwater fish species.

Author Page

Billy Grinslott – Kinsey Marie Books

Copyright, All Rights Reserved

ISBN – 9781968228651

Thanks